# The Spelling Bee

Written by Shagufta K Iqbal
Illustrated by Hamnah Rizwan

**Collins**

# 1 Hana

Things had been slowly building up for a long time, but the breaking point came on a Monday morning at the start of the summer term. Monday was Hana's favourite day of the week, because she had Art and Science at school. She liked the colours, textures and formulas that these subjects required. Hana was very proud of her artistic and scientific skills!

But despite being so talented, Hana still struggled to do her shoelaces. So, every morning, her older brother, Adil, would help her tie them. Sometimes he would show her the bunny ears method – her favourite method. (Hana had a lot of favourite things.) Sometimes Adil showed her the helicopter method, and sometimes he would invent his own special method. He would explain each one with sound effects and in funny voices to make her laugh.

Hana's brother was excellent at acting, and his favourite lesson was Drama. Adil was also the most excellent Breaktime Buddy, helping younger children in their school with games during lunchtimes. Hana was very proud of her big brother. Dad said they were two peas in a pod, and Mum called them The Awesome Twosome.

Adil was three years older than Hana, and they both had their birthdays in August. Their parents would plan an exciting joint day out each year to celebrate. This year, for Hana's seventh birthday and Adil's tenth birthday, they went to a theme park. They both picked the same flavour of ice cream and loved the same rides – although Adil had to let Hana squeeze his arm on the scary ones.

But on that particular Monday morning, Adil didn't do the funny voices. They were both in the hallway but, while Adil was ready for school with his backpack on, Hana was not ready. Her shoelaces dangled like the tentacles of a slippery octopus.

"You're seven now, so you should know how to do them by yourself!" Adil huffed.

Hana didn't expect Adil to be so grumpy. She tried her best to make him come out of his bad mood by making silly faces (which would normally make him burst out laughing). But today he just turned his back to her and didn't laugh, not even a tiny bit. It was as though her brother was a complete stranger. Mum asked Adil to help Hana as she was busy packing the car, but he wasn't listening. Dad was busy making their lunches.

"Help your sister, please, Adil," Dad chipped in.

Adil groaned, and reluctantly tied Hana's shoelaces, making it seem like it was such a chore. Then, without saying a word, he stormed out of the door and stood next to the car. Hana quietly followed him, while mum was putting things in the car boot.

"I hope your first Spelling Bee practice goes well, Adil!" Dad shouted encouragingly from the front door. "I know you'll try your best."

Adil just grunted, with his arms crossed over his chest. Hana wondered what had happened to change her brother so much. Who was this scowling imposter?

# 2 Adil

When Adil arrived at school, the classroom was unusually warm and the sun shone brightly through the window. Even with the windows open, it felt stifling and hot.

Adil placed all his things in a neat order on his desk:

a sharp pencil,
a shiny silver sharpener,
a clear plastic ruler,
and a new red book with his name and
'Spelling Bee Practice' written on it.

Mr Malik was standing at the front of the class, bouncing on the balls of his feet.

"OK, everyone, are we ready for our first weekly Spelling Bee practice session? It's adverbs and adjectives today!" He noticed that Adil was all set up at his desk and gave him an impressed nod.

"Excellent, Adil!" he exclaimed. "Chop chop, Einstein Class." He clapped his hands and looked very excited.

Mr Malik had organised for all the local schools to come together for a Spelling Bee competition at the end of term. Each school had to nominate a group of students from their oldest class to compete. The Spelling Bee wasn't like a normal written spelling test. Instead, competitors were told a word and they had to say the correct spelling out loud in front of an audience. If they got it wrong, they were eliminated until there was one winner.

The whole school was very excited, with the younger classes making colourful banners for the final event.

Everyone in Einstein Class had to prepare for the Spelling Bee. Every Monday leading up to the competition, Mr Malik would select children at random to stand at the front of the room and say spellings out loud. Then, the week before competition day, the class would choose five students to represent their school.

While Einstein Class got themselves ready for the spelling practice, groaning and trying to sneakily take one last peek at today's word list, Mr Malik paced the front of the classroom. He had lots of energy and was always clicking his pens in his shirt pocket. Sometimes the pens would leak ink onto his shirt and he would pretend he had been hit with a paintball. He would drop to the floor in a very dramatic way. Everyone liked Mr Malik.

Mr Malik chose two of Adil's classmates to begin the practice session. He held his finger out and said very loudly and slowly, "Number one: Curiously."

Adil was relieved that he wasn't picked first. But he knew it would be his turn at some point, so he decided to practise in his head.

"Cur-i-ous-ly," Mr Malik repeated, drawing out the syllables.

Adil felt his heart beating and beads of sweat appearing in his hair line. He took a deep breath and wiped his forehead with his shaking hand.

He tried very hard to picture the word. But the letters began moving around in his brain: they wiggled and changed order, they jumped and shapeshifted, merging and splitting.

He squeezed his eyes shut and tried really hard to remember what the word looked like when he had been revising.

C U R Y O S L E E

Adil's head hurt. His stomach began to ache, and he felt a sickening feeling rising in his throat. Just when he couldn't take it anymore, he put his hand up.

Mr Malik looked at him, surprised.

"I don't feel well," Adil said, his face flushed red.

Mr Malik wrote him a note to say he could go to the medical room. As Adil made his way to the door, he noticed his friend Georgi giving him a look, as though she didn't believe him. Everyone must have thought he was just trying to get out of the Spelling Bee practice, but the truth was Adil felt awful and he couldn't explain why.

# 3 Hana

The next week, things got even worse. Hana barely heard a word from Adil over the weekend. She noticed that her brother was spending more and more time on his own. Usually, he would spend all breaktime playing football with the rest of his class. But these days, Adil was wearing a frown on his face all the time. He was sharp and snappy when anyone spoke to him, and he'd lost all his usual playfulness.

In the playground, Georgi, who was a Breaktime Buddy like Adil, was teaching Hana a new skipping rope game. This was Hana's favourite breaktime activity. As they skipped, Georgi mentioned that Adil was feeling unwell again in class, like he did last Monday. But Mr Malik said he had to finish the Spelling Bee practice this time, and if he still felt unwell afterwards, he could go to the medical room.

"Adil seemed annoyed that he wasn't allowed to leave straight away," Georgi continued. "And he acted very strangely when it was his turn to go to the front of the class. He didn't say anything at all when Mr Malik gave him his word to spell."

"But he was revising in his room all weekend," said Hana, feeling confused. Adil seemed grumpy, but he wasn't unwell at all at home.

Georgi agreed. "This just isn't like him."

Hana began to worry even more. She felt like she was a box that was about to burst open as it was too full. She wasn't the only one who had noticed that Adil was becoming very snappy. He was a different person from the brother she had always known and loved.

Later that day, Hana and Adil were very quiet in the car home. Mum tried to make conversation and sang along to the radio. Hana joined in with the singing. Singing to Mum's music was another one of Hana's favourite things.

But Adil did not join in, and he only responded to questions with one-word statements. Mum asked him if everything was OK. Adil just shrugged and said nothing. Hana noticed that Mum didn't force him to explain. Instead, she just looked at him with furrowed eyebrows and tight lips.

When they got home, Adil went straight to his room and closed the door. With no one to play with, Hana was by herself with her worries. What was making Adil become so distant?

# 4 Adil

A few weeks later, Adil's parents were called into school for a meeting because his behaviour had become worse. He had been sent to the Headteacher, Mr Olu's office for the third week in a row. He had refused to set up his desk for class, and had then tripped Georgi up as she walked to the front of the class for her turn in the Spelling Bee practice. Georgi felt hurt by Adil's actions, Mr Malik was very shocked at Adil's behaviour and his parents were deeply disappointed.

But the meeting didn't change things. In fact, Adil's trips to Mr Olu's office became more regular. Every day for the rest of the week, Adil was sent out of class again and told to sit outside the office in one of the uncomfortable chairs. He would watch the clock ticking away the time until lunch. Then, in the afternoon, he would be allowed back into class on the promise of better behaviour.

However, on Friday, when Adil walked into Mr Olu's office, he was surprised to find Miss Williams, the deputy headteacher. She was standing over a potted plant and was watering it with a small purple watering can.

"Hello Adil. Come in and take a seat." She gestured to the chair opposite Mr Olu's desk.

Adil was even more surprised because he would usually be sent to sit *outside* the office.

"Could you please continue watering these plants? I have some marking to do."

Miss Williams told Adil how much to water each plant and then sat at the desk to get on with her marking. Then she explained that Mr Olu was on a course, and that she would be taking over his role for the next few weeks while he was away.

As Adil went around the office tending to the many plants, he noticed his muscles becoming more relaxed and he felt a bit less angry. Miss Williams had stickers on all the plant pots: Adil realised she had given them all names.

By the time he had completed the task, Miss Williams had finished her marking. She was sitting in the reading corner, looking through the bookcase.

"This is my favourite story," she said, picking out a book with a giant plant growing high into the sky on the cover. "Can you read it to me, please?"

Adil began to feel queasy. He liked Miss Williams, but he didn't want to read to her. He was afraid that he would get the words wrong.

But Miss Williams was very persistent. They sat in the reading corner and Adil began. As he read, Adil found that the letters tumbled and fell on the page, leaping and merging together. Adil struggled to find the meaning in the words and to put the story together. He started to feel a quiet rage growing inside him. His chest felt like a hot air balloon, growing bigger and bigger, until he felt he might explode.

Why did everyone else find this so easy?

Adil wished that lunchtime would hurry up.
But Miss Williams gently encouraged him. "Go ahead Adil, what does it say?"

His mouth felt dry and his cheeks flushed red. He waited for Miss Williams to tell him off for getting it wrong. But Miss Williams, sensing that he felt anxious, softly took the book from him.

"Do you know why I like people to read to me?"

Adil shook his lowered head.

She continued, "Stories make me feel alive and free, but reading can be quite tricky for me."

Miss Williams put the book back on the shelf, smiled and said, "Do you want to know an interesting fact about me? I have something called dyslexia. It affects people differently. But for me, it just shows how we all learn in our own way."

Adil was shocked as Miss Williams explained how words on a page leap and jump when she tries to read them. She explained how sometimes her words get muddled up.

Adil knew exactly what Miss Williams meant, because a similar thing happened to him too. He suddenly felt safe and accepted, but he was still too embarrassed to tell Miss Williams out loud.

# 5 Adil

The next Monday, instead of waiting for Adil to misbehave, Miss Williams called him directly to her office. He was relieved that he didn't have to do the Spelling Bee practice, but at the same time, he felt anxious and wondered why Miss Williams had called him out of class.

He remembered hearing his mum talking quietly on the phone with Miss Williams last Friday. As much as Adil had tried to listen in, he couldn't make out what they were saying. He knew it must have been about him. He felt very alone in that moment, as though no one understood how he was feeling.

He didn't want to behave badly, but he really didn't want to be made fun of during Spelling Bee practice. It was affecting him so much that he didn't even feel like taking part in Drama anymore, his favourite lesson.

"Oh Adil, just the person I wanted to see," said Miss Williams brightly, as she handed him the watering can and took a seat at the desk. Adil watered the plants, just as he had been directed to do last time. Once he had finished, Miss Williams asked him to sit at the desk opposite her. She was drinking a flowery herbal tea and offered him a delicious orange squash.

"Shall we do this activity sheet?" she asked after taking a big slurp of her tea. "Now let's see, what pattern do you think goes next?"

Adil was so relieved that Miss Williams wasn't asking him to read to her again that he jumped at the chance to do the activity sheet. The activities were fun! They looked at patterns and shapes, words, numbers and sequences. While doing the activity sheet, they both realised that Adil was an expert at anagrams! With all the letters jumping around on the page, Adil was very quick at working out the hidden word the letters made. Miss Williams was impressed – she found anagrams very tricky herself.

Once they had finished, Miss Williams explained to Adil, "I had to do an activity sheet like this one when I was trying to learn if I had dyslexia or not. Do you remember what I spoke to you about last week?"

Adil nodded. In fact, he couldn't stop thinking about what Miss Williams had said to him about everyone having their own way of learning.

"Well, your parents and I think that there may be some similarities between your way of learning and mine. We want to offer you support and see if we can make reading and writing a little easier for you. I have some helpful tips and tricks that I have learned over the years. Would you be interested in knowing some of my top-secret learning strategies?"

More strategies! Adil felt excited. He had already boosted his confidence by solving anagrams. But it was even better that Miss Williams would teach him new and fun things. She had changed the text font on his activity sheets, so he could read them more easily. Adil was also booked in to take an eye-test before his dyslexia assessment, which was going to help him understand how he learns new information.

Adil felt like a plant that had sprung into life. It was as though he had been sitting on a windowsill for a long time, and finally someone had come along and poured some refreshing water over him.

# 6 Hana

A few weeks later, it was finally the last week of term! The week started with a big day. Hana did her laces all by herself! Not only that, but it was the day of the Spelling Bee Competition.

Adil had been practising anagrams for ages. He had helped Hana to understand what an anagram was, although she still got a bit confused. But her brother told her:

"That's OK, we all have our own way of learning. Everyone has their own strengths."

"Like art and science," Hana beamed proudly.

"Exactly! Like art and science," Adil laughed. "But there's nothing wrong with asking for help when you're struggling to understand other things."

That Monday morning, as Hana sat in the front row of the assembly hall, she looked at her neatly-tied laces. She hadn't used the bunny ears method, or the helicopter method. She used her own special Hana method. Everyone at home was very proud.

Then Hana looked up and saw Adil standing by the stage, next to some of his classmates and children from other local schools.

Hana felt nervous for Adil, as she waited for him to come on stage. Adil was representing Einstein Class in a new category. After speaking with Miss Williams and Adil a few weeks ago, Mr Malik had decided to add an anagram round to the competition. And Adil was chosen to represent his class!

As he walked onto the stage, Hana saw Adil take a big deep breath. She waved at him encouragingly, and he gave her a quick smile. Then he began the anagram challenge with a confidence that let Hana know she had got her brother back.

# Changing feelings

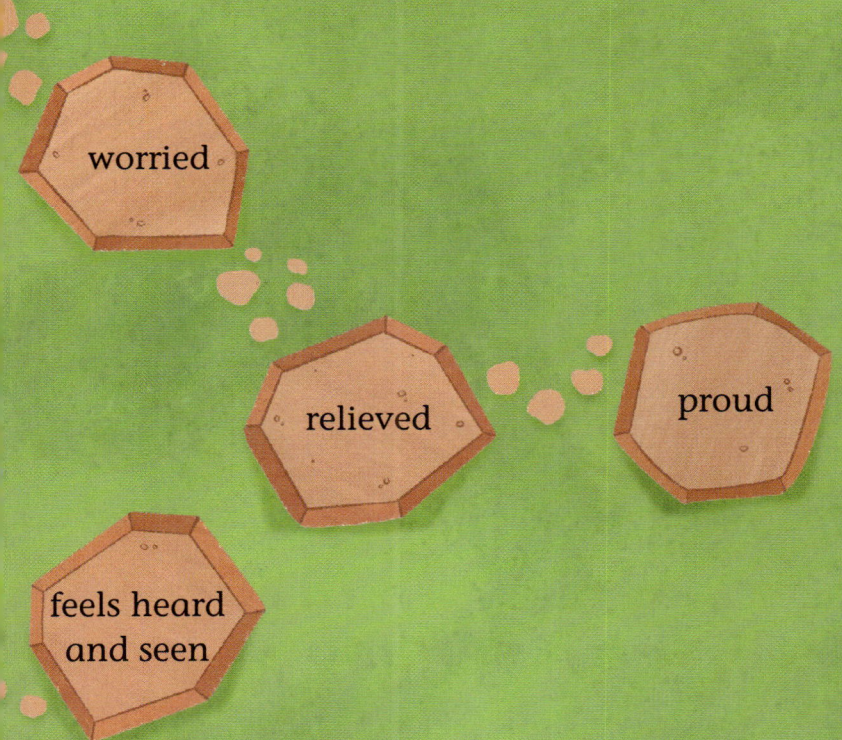

# Ideas for reading

Written by Gill Matthews
*Primary Literacy Consultant*

**Reading objectives:**
- draw on what they already know or on background information and vocabulary provided by the teacher
- make inferences on the basis of what is being said and done
- answer and ask questions

**Spoken language objectives:**
- articulate and justify answers, arguments and opinions
- participate in discussions, presentations, performances, role play, improvisations and debates

**Curriculum links:** Relationships education: Respectful relationships

**Word count:** 3068

**Interest words:** huffed, groaned, reluctantly, stormed, grunted, scowling

## Build a context for reading

- Ask children to look at the front cover of the book and to read the title. Explore their understanding of what a *Spelling Bee* is.
- Discuss how children think they would feel if they took part in a Spelling Bee.
- Read the back cover blurb. Discuss what might happen in the story.

## Understand and apply reading strategies

- Read pp2–9 aloud, using meaning, punctuation and dialogue to help you read with appropriate expression.
- Discuss the characters who have been introduced in this opening chapter. Explore what children think the characters are like.
- Encourage children to speculate why Adil is behaving differently.
- Give children the opportunity to read the rest of the book. Pause at the end of each chapter to discuss how Adil is feeling. Ensure children understand the meaning of *anagram*. Use the illustration on p37 to support understanding.